Famous Artists

Get to Know
Norman Rockwell

Charlotte Taylor

Enslow Publishing
101 W. 23rd Street
Suite 240
New York, NY 10011
USA
enslow.com

Published in 2016 by Enslow Publishing, LLC
101 W. 23rd Street, Suite 240, New York, NY 10011

Copyright © 2016 by Enslow Publishing, LLC
All rights reserved.

No part of this book may be reproduced by any means
without the written permission of the publisher.

Library of Congress Cataloging-in-Publication Data
Taylor, Charlotte, 1978- author.
 Get to know Norman Rockwell / Charlotte Taylor.
     pages cm. — (Famous artists)
 Includes bibliographical references and index.
 Summary: "Describes the life and work of iconic American painter Norman Rockwell"— Provided by publisher.
 ISBN 978-0-7660-7238-1 (library binding)
 ISBN 968-0-7660-7236-7 (pbk)
 ISBN 978-0-7660-7237-4 (6 pk)
1. Rockwell, Norman, 1894-1978—Juvenile literature. 2. Painters—United States—Biography—Juvenile literature. 3. Illustrators—United States—Biography—Juvenile literature. I. Title.
 ND237.R68T39 2016
 759.13—dc23
 [B]
                              2015029907

Printed in the United States of America

To Our Readers: We have done our best to make sure all website addresses in this book were active and appropriate when we went to press. However, the author and the publisher have no control over and assume no liability for the material available on those websites or any websites they may link to. Any comments or suggestions can be sent by e-mail to customerservice@enslow.com.

Photo Credits: Cover, pp. 1, 4 John Bryson/The LIFE Images Collection/Getty Images; throughout book Rudchenko Liliia/Shutterstock.com (painting background), Mostovyi Sergii Igorevich/Shutterstock.com (palate and brushes dingbat), foxie/Shutterstock.com (brushstrokes), rzstudio/Shutterstock.com (paint brush) p. 7 Museum of the City of New York/Byron Collection/Archive Photos/Getty Images; p. 9 National Portrait Gallery, Smithsonian Institution/Art Resource; pp. 11, 36 Library of Congress, Prints and Photographs Division; p 13 The New York Historical Society/Archive Photos/Getty Images; p. 15 The Art Archive at Art Resource, NY; p. 18 Library of Congress, Prints and Photographs Division; p. 20 © Albert Knapp / Alamy Stock Photo; p. 23 Heritage/heritage/Superstock; p. 24 Apic/Hulton Archive/Getty Images; p. 27 © American Photo Archive / Alamy Stock Photo; p. 30 © Pictorial Press Ltd / Alamy Stock Photo; p. 33 John Greim/LightRocket/Getty Images; p. 35 © epa european pressphoto agency b.v. / Alamy Stock Photo; p. 38 John Bryson/The LIFE Images Collection/Getty Images; p. 40 © PLStamps / Alamy Stock Photo; p 42 © CastlePhotography / Alamy Stock Photo; p. 44 © Terry Smith Images / Alamy Stock Photo

Contents

Chapter 1
America's Artist 5

Chapter 2
Learning to Draw 10

Chapter 3
Success at the *Post* 17

Chapter 4
Rockwell and the War........... 26

Chapter 5
Changing Times.................. 32

Chapter 6
Remembering Rockwell 39

Timeline............................ 45
Glossary............................ 46
Learn More 47
Index............................... 48

Chapter 1

America's Artist

Norman Rockwell painted ordinary people doing ordinary things. By doing this, he told the story of America. Many people call Rockwell the most famous and beloved painter in the world.

Rockwell painted seven days a week for most of his life. He created nearly four thousand pictures, including eight hundred magazine covers and ads for more than 150 companies. His most famous paintings were 324 magazine covers. Millions of people saw his work month after month, year after year. Many years after his death, people still see his paintings in museums, magazines, books, and even on stamps.

Norman Rockwell's paintings honor the best qualities of the country he loved. They make people feel that the world is a safe and friendly place.

Get to Know Norman Rockwell

Not everybody thinks Norman Rockwell is a great artist. Many art critics have said that his pictures are rather silly and not serious art. They have said that a real artist does not make as much money as Rockwell did. But Rockwell did not paint for them. He painted for regular people.

Norman wanted to create a world of happiness in his pictures that was unlike his sad, sometimes lonely childhood. Although he said his family was "a nice family," he did not feel like he fit in.

Growing Up

Norman Percevel Rockwell was born on February 3, 1894. His family lived on the fifth floor of an apartment building in New York City. His father, Jarvis Waring Rockwell, was a quiet, stern man. He worked in the office of a textile company. Nancy Hill Rockwell was a homemaker who was sick in bed most of the time. Mr. Rockwell fussed over his wife quite a bit, but he was not as loving with his sons. He treated Norman and his older brother, Jarvis, like grown-ups. Their home was usually quiet and serious.

The neighborhood the Rockwells lived in was a bit rough. There were street gangs who got into fights. The children played games, such as tag and touch football, on the sidewalks and in the alleys. The kids who were strong and good at games

America's Artist

Rockwell was born in New York City in 1896. This photo was taken around the same time.

Get to Know Norman Rockwell

were the most popular. Norman's brother, Jarvis, was very good at games. He was always picked for teams.

Norman, however, was clumsy and his feet turned in. He was forced to wear special heavy shoes to fix his feet. Norman was the slowest runner on the block and did not often join the other kids in their games.

Norman did not like the way he looked. He was so pale that his mother nicknamed him "Snow-in-the-Face." He had skinny "spaghetti arms," and his Adam's apple stuck out. The other children called him "Moony" because of the round rimless glasses he wore.

But Norman did have a special talent. He sure could draw! He started drawing when he was about four or five, and he never stopped. His father and his grandfather, an English artist who painted animals and birds, both inspired him. "I think I've always wanted to be an artist," Rockwell said many times. "I certainly can't remember ever wanting to be anything else."

America's Artist

A young Rockwell at his easel.

Chapter 2

Learning to Draw

Mr. Rockwell used to sketch copies of pictures from magazines. Norman like to watch him. The two spent many evenings drawing together at the dining room table. Mr. Rockwell also read stories aloud to the family. Norman drew pictures of the characters as he imagined them. Norman practiced his drawing skills at home and at school. His classmates and teachers loved looking at Norman's sketches.

When Norman's eighth-grade teacher allowed him to decorate the chalkboards with huge drawings, he was thrilled. Rockwell remembered his first "one-man displays" with happiness and pride. The praise he got made him feel sure he could do whatever it took to become an artist.

Norman worked at part-time jobs to save up money for art school. He delivered mail on his bicycle. He taught sketching to future actress Ethel Barrymore. He was even an "extra" in

Learning to Draw

Rockwell as a young man.

Get to Know Norman Rockwell

some performances at the Metropolitan Opera. Norman earned enough money to take classes at the Chase School of Fine and Applied Art in New York.

Art Student

The Rockwells had moved to a town north of the city, so Norman had to take a long trip by trolley and subway to get to the school. Twice a week he made the four-hour round-trip journey.

Norman soon realized that he did not have enough time for high school, art classes, and work. He dropped out of high school to enter the National Academy of Design in New York. Norman's parents were disappointed. They wanted him to finish school and get a "real job." They thought most artists were poor. But Norman took his career seriously. He knew he could do well as an artist.

At the National Academy, Norman drew for eight hours a day six days a week. It was good training, but it was tiring. Norman switched over to the Art Students League. It was a better place for him.

Over the next three years, Norman studied art. He decided that he wanted to become an illustrator. Illustrations are pictures that all people can understand. They are sold to companies and publishers and printed in magazines,

Learning to Draw

This is the National Academy of Design in New York City, where Rockwell studied art.

Get to Know Norman Rockwell

storybooks, and calendars. When Norman was in school, some illustrators were so well known they were treated like movie stars.

Working as an Illustrator

Norman Rockwell's first illustrating job was for a book called *Tell Me Why Stories.* He was paid $150 for twelve pictures. Then he drew pictures for a handbook for *Boy's Life*, a Boy Scout magazine. The editor was so pleased with the pictures that he made Rockwell the magazine's art director. It was 1913 and Norman was just nineteen years old. Over the next sixty years, Rockwell would paint the covers for almost every Boy Scout calendar.

Rockwell also did some illustrations for advertising companies. He painted ads for toothpaste, cereal, soda, and cough medicine. He received a lot of money for his work. Rockwell was proud that he was becoming popular, but he was not yet satisfied.

At the time, the best thing that could happen for an illustrator was to be chosen to paint a cover for the *Saturday Evening Post.* Millions of people all over the world used to read this weekly magazine. Rockwell dreamed of being a cover artist but for a long time he was too nervous to try. He was afraid the editor would laugh at him. In 1916 a friend finally got

Learning to Draw

Rockwell works on an early *Saturday Evening Post* cover.

Get to Know Norman Rockwell

him to take five pictures to the *Saturday Evening Post* office. Rockwell was so nervous that he almost turned around and went home when he got to the *Post* building.

Luckily, the magazine's editors liked the pictures. They bought two of his paintings and asked him to do three more.

"Wow!" Rockwell later said about that time. "A cover on the *Post*! I had arrived."

Chapter 3

Success at the Post

From the very first cover for the *Saturday Evening Post*, Rockwell's art was a hit. His first cover was called *Boy With Baby Carriage*. It shows an unhappy boy pushing a baby carriage past his friends, who are running off to play baseball. The illustration was very well liked. Rockwell did many more covers. Readers of the magazine were delighted by his pictures. More people bought the magazine when there was a Rockwell painting on the cover. That made the *Post*'s publishers very happy.

Rockwell's *Post* covers were sometimes funny scenes about childhood. One was of a surprised little boy who discovers a Santa Claus suit in his parents' dresser. Another was of a girl with a black eye smiling outside the principal's office. Another was of some boys running past a "No Swimming" sign, who

Get to Know Norman Rockwell

Helping Mother (1917, Library of Congress, Washington, DC). Rockwell painted many covers for magazines other than the *Saturday Evening Post*.

Success at the Post

look like they have just been swimming. Other covers showed families, couples in love, and animals.

Years later, millions of *Post* readers voted for their favorite Rockwell cover. They chose *Saying Grace*, a painting of an old woman and young boy praying in a diner. It was a simple scene about ordinary people, but it touched people's hearts.

Rockwell's best subjects were "ordinary folks"—people who were not special, people whom you might see every day. But he also painted famous people, such as presidents and movie stars.

Posing for Rockwell

Since his days in art school, Rockwell had used real people as models. He asked neighborhood children to pose for him. He paid them fifty cents an hour. The kids liked the money, but the job was hard. It was not easy to sit still in the same position for hours. Sometimes they had to keep a smile or frown on their face or hold an uncomfortable position for a long time.

Norman placed stacks of nickels on the table to show the children how much they had earned so far. "Here's an extra nickel," he would say to keep his models cheerful. Although he was very serious about his painting, he joked and played music for the kids.

Get to Know Norman Rockwell

Saying Grace (1951, Private Collection). This cover was voted the favorite of *Post* readers. The painting shows a woman and a little boy in a diner praying before they eat their meal.

Success at the *Post*

Art Smarts

In the 1930s, Rockwell began working with a camera. First, he would set up a scene that he wanted to paint and he would take several pictures of it. Then, he would paint while looking at the photographs rather than at live models. This way, he could paint without making people stay in one position for too long.

In these early years, the children and adults who modeled for him were proud to see their faces on the covers of magazines. It made all the hard work of posing worthwhile. Later in his career, Rockwell used photographs instead of live models.

Creating the Cover

Norman Rockwell's illustrations were always created carefully. First, he had to come up with an idea. He thought and doodled and read and looked around until he found one he liked. Then, he made small sketches. He shared them with the editor or

Get to Know Norman Rockwell

Important Business (1919). Rockwell painted many pictures of everyday activities, like golfing.

Success at the Post

art director, who also had to like them. Next, Rockwell would choose his models. He made large black-and-white drawings of them.

Then, it was time to add color. Rockwell sometimes had to test with many different colors until he was happy with what he had. Finally, he painted with oil paints on canvas. When the painting was done, it was delivered to the magazine. The magazine then printed thousands and thousands of copies for all the world to see.

Rockwell's Loves

Norman Rockwell's life as an illustrator was very successful. His love life, however, had its ups and downs. Rockwell married Irene O'Connor in 1916, soon after his first *Saturday Evening Post* cover was accepted. Irene liked to party and play, while Norman was much happier working. The couple divorced in 1929.

The following year, Rockwell met a schoolteacher named Mary Barstow. They fell in love and were married. Norman and Mary were happy together. They had three sons—Jarvis, Thomas, and Peter.

The Rockwell family moved to Arlington, Vermont, when the boys were young. The small town was a much better place for Rockwell. He had been feeling less confident about his artwork.

Get to Know Norman Rockwell

Rockwell works in his studio in Vermont.

Success at the *Post*

Also, he had been unhappy living in a big city and preferred the quiet of the countryside.

Rockwell's new friends and neighbors were happy when the artist moved into town. Many of them could not wait to be models for Rockwell's illustrations. His art began to include scenes of life in a small town. In Vermont, Rockwell would paint many of his most popular pictures.

Chapter 4

Rockwell and the War

It was the middle of the night and Normal Rockwell was wide awake. He had just had the most wonderful idea. He jumped out of bed, too excited to sleep.

It was 1942 and the country was fighting in a terrible war called World War II. American and British soldiers were fighting against Germany, Italy, and Japan. Rockwell was very patriotic—he loved his country a great deal. He wanted to help America, but he was too old to fight. Years earlier, during World War I, Rockwell had joined the US Navy. He drew portraits of navy men that they would send home to their wives. Now, he decided to use his art once again to help people feel better during a war.

The *Four Freedoms*

President Franklin Roosevelt had spoken to the nation about four basic freedoms that people had. "The first is freedom of

Rockwell and the War

This poster of Rockwell's *The Homecoming* helped to raise money for the American effort in World War II.

Get to Know Norman Rockwell

speech," the president said. "The second is freedom of every person to worship God in his own way. The third is freedom from want. The fourth is freedom from fear."

Norman Rockwell decided to show these four freedoms the way average Americans lived them. The idea came to him at three o'clock in the morning. Rockwell rode his bicycle over to a friend's house. He woke him up and told him the plan. The friend agreed that it was a wonderful idea. Rockwell went back home to begin.

A few days later, Rockwell drew sketches of the four freedoms and took them to Washington, DC. The people in the government were not interested. They told Rockwell they wanted "real artists" for this war, not illustrators.

Rockwell was disappointed. He left Washington. On his way home, he stopped in at the *Saturday Evening Post* office. The new editor, Ben Hibbs, liked the four drawings so much, he wanted them as covers for his magazine. Rockwell was thrilled. He promised to finish them in a few months.

The paintings turned out to be much more difficult than he expected. Rockwell struggled for six months to get them just right. Finally, he was satisfied. The four paintings were done.

The first painting, *Freedom of Speech*, shows a man standing tall in a room as his neighbors listen to him speak his mind. *Freedom of Worship* shows a group of people praying. The people

Rockwell and the War

Art Smarts

If you look closely at Rockwell's paintings, you will notice lots of details. Every object has a lot of little things to notice about it. How did he manage to come up with such realistic details? One of his tricks was that he used good props and costumes. Rockwell had a large collection of costumes for his models to wear—but not Halloween costumes. He kept such things as old, worn blue jeans or old hats. He wanted his models to look like real people. All his props were used items, because he felt they would look right only if they had been used by real people.

Get to Know Norman Rockwell

Four Freedoms (1943, Norman Rockwell Museum, Stockbridge, MA). (Clockwise from top left—*Freedom of Speech, Freedom of Religion, Freedom From Want, Freedom From Fear*) Rockwell got the idea for these paintings from a 1941 speech by President Franklin D. Roosevelt. They were so popular that the government had them made into posters so people could buy them.

Rockwell and the War

are of different faiths and races. For *Freedom From Want*, Rockwell painted a happy family at a Thanksgiving table. In *Freedom From Fear*, parents are tucking their children safely into bed.

Success and Loss

The paintings were published in the *Post*. They were a tremendous success. The United States Treasury Department took them on a traveling show. Rockwell's series helped raise nearly $133 million for the war. Over one million people saw the paintings. Seventy thousand wrote to Rockwell to say how much they loved them. Millions of prints were sold around the world. It was Norman Rockwell's biggest triumph. He was more admired, and more famous than ever.

A few days after Norman Rockwell sent the finished *Four Freedoms* to the *Post,* a terrible thing happened. His studio caught fire and burned down. He lost many paintings and sketches. However, he was grateful that the *Four Freedoms* paintings were safe. He built a new studio and got back to work.

Chapter 5

Changing Times

In 1953 Norman's wife, Mary, was not well. The Rockwells decided to move to Stockbridge, Massachusetts. The town was closer to her doctors. While Mary was sick, Rockwell and his son Tom wrote *My Adventures as an Illustrator,* a book that told Rockwell's story in his own words.

Six years after the move, Mary died. Rockwell was sad and lonely without his wife. After a couple of years, he met and married Molly Punderson, a retired teacher. Rockwell's third marriage was also a good one. He and Molly traveled around the world. Rockwell painted many important people on his trip.

In 1963, forty-seven years after his first cover, Rockwell stopped working for the *Saturday Evening Post.* He was not happy with the way the new staff treated him. He was ready for a change.

Changing Times

Rockwell liked his life in Vermont, but was ready for a change. His home and studio in Massachusetts was later turned into a museum.

Get to Know Norman Rockwell

A New America

Other magazines asked Rockwell to illustrate pictures of the changing nation. Rockwell made an illustration for *Look* magazine. It was called *The Problem We All Live With.* It shows a sweet, little African-American girl walking into an all-white school. She is protected by soldiers. At that time, a new law said that black children and white children should go to the same schools. Many people, especially in the South, had a hard time accepting that idea. Black people and white people had always been kept apart. With one picture, Rockwell was able to tell the story of this powerful argument that was going on in the United States.

Rockwell also made paintings about a black family moving into a white neighborhood. He painted the *Apollo 11* space landing. His illustrations had told the story of the United States, from people riding on horse-and-buggies to a man walking on the moon.

In July 1976, America celebrated its two hundredth birthday. Rockwell painted a picture of himself wrapping a ribbon around the Liberty Bell. It was Norman Rockwell's last magazine cover. He was eighty-two years old. He had been illustrating covers for sixty years.

The following year, President Gerald Ford honored Norman Rockwell with the Presidential Medal of Freedom—the nation's highest peacetime award.

Changing Times

Rockwell did hundreds of covers for the *Saturday Evening Post*. Many are on display in museums. Others are in private collections and are worth thousands of dollars.

Get to Know Norman Rockwell

This is Rockwell's studio in Massachusetts.

Changing Times

Norman Rockwell once said to a friend, "Maybe the secret to so many artists living so long is that every painting is a new adventure. So, you see, they're always looking ahead to something new and exciting."

Norman Rockwell always looked forward to his next idea. He always hoped his next painting would be his best one.

Get to Know Norman Rockwell

This photo, from 1975 shows Rockwell and his third wife, Molly, looking at one of Rockwell's framed sketches from their travels.

Chapter 6

Remembering Rockwell

By 1978 Rockwell had grown weak and tired. He had stopped painting, but he still drew with paper and pencil. The artist died on November 8 at the age of eighty-four. His last picture was sitting on his easel when he passed away.

Rockwell was buried in Stockbridge Cemetery. His friends and neighbors said he was a warm person with a gentle humor. He was a good man as well as a great illustrator.

The Art Lives On

Rockwell's paintings now hang in important museums, such as the Metropolitan Museum of Art in New York and the National Portrait Gallery in Washington, D.C. Rockwell exhibits are shown around the world. The Arlington Gallery in Vermont has a popular Norman Rockwell exhibition.

Get to Know Norman Rockwell

Triple Self-Portrait (1959, Norman Rockwell Museum, Stockbridge, MA). In 1994 Rockwell was honored by the US Postal Service with a 29-cent stamp showing one of his most well-known paintings.

Remembering Rockwell

Art Smarts

Take a very close look at *Triple Self-Portrait*. Notice the four pictures on the right side of the easel. They are self-portraits done by other famous artists: Durer, van Rijn, Picasso, and Van Gogh. All of these artists were known for painting self-portraits. (Rockwell only painted two other self-portraits in his life.) Rockwell was likely poking fun at himself by comparing himself to these master artists.

Get to Know Norman Rockwell

Golden Rule, made in 1961, is on display at the Norman Rockwell Museum in Stockbridge, Massachusetts. Thousands of tourists visit the museum every year to see Rockwell's work, studio, and where he lived.

Remembering Rockwell

The largest collection of Rockwell's work is in Stockbridge, Massachusetts. The museum contains hundreds of his paintings and drawings. Rockwell's entire red barn studio was moved to the grounds near the museum. His paintbrushes, paints, and easel are set up inside. The museum also contains some of Rockwell's personal things and some of his props. Thousands of people visit the Norman Rockwell Museum every year.

Norman Rockwell painted the stories of ordinary people, but his pictures were never ordinary. They made people feel special. They gave people hope. Norman Rockwell showed America at its best.

Get to Know Norman Rockwell

Rosie the Riveter (1943, Crystal Bridges Museum of American Art, Bentonville, AR). This is one of Rockwell's most beloved images. His work is still some of the most popular in American history.

Timeline

1894—Norman Percevel Rockwell is born in New York City on February 3.
1909—Attends National Academy of Design.
1910—Attends Art Students League.
1913—Becomes art director at *Boys' Life*.
1916—Gets first *Saturday Evening Post* cover; marries Irene O'Connor.
1929—Divorces Irene O'Connor.
1930—Marries Mary Barstow.
1939—Moves to Arlington, Vermont.
1943—*Four Freedoms* is published in the *Post*; studio burns to the ground.
1951—Paints *Saying Grace.*
1953—Moves to Stockbridge, Massachusetts.
1959—His wife, Mary, dies.
1960—Publishes life story.
1961—Marries Molly Punderson.
1963—Last *Post* cover printed.
1964—*Look* magazine cover published: *The Problem We All Live With.*
1965—Paints man's travels to the moon for *Look* magazine.
1976—Last magazine cover appears on *American Artist.*
1977—Receives Presidential Medal of Freedom.
1978—Dies at age eighty-four.
1993—Norman Rockwell Museum opens in Stockbridge, Massachusetts.
2008—Rockwell is named the official state artist of Massachusetts.
2013—*Saying Grace* is sold for $46 million, a new record for Rockwell.

Glossary

art critics—People who give opinions about art.

canvas—A strong piece of cloth artists paint on.

editor—A person who decides what goes into a magazine or book.

exhibit—A show or display.

gallery—A place where works of art are shown.

illustrator—A person who draws pictures that are published in books or magazines.

model—A person who poses for a painting or photo.

ordinary—Common, everyday, not special.

patriotic—Very proud of one's country.

pose—To stay very still to be painted or photographed.

prop—An object used in a play, movie, or other form of art.

series—A group of paintings that belong together in a certain order.

sketches—Quick drawings.

textile—Cloth.

Learn More

Books

Brooks, Susie. *Get Into Art: People.* Boston: Kingfisher, 2013.

Finch, Christopher. *Norman Rockwell: 332 Magazine Covers.* New York: Abbeville Press, 2013.

Frisch-Schmoll, Joy. *Portraits.* Mankato, MN: Creative Paperbacks, 2013.

Websites

The Norman Rockwell Museum at Stockbridge
www.nrm.org
Read a brief biography of Rockwell and get information about the museum, in Stockbridge, Massachusetts. The museum holds the largest collection of Rockwell's work.

Norman Rockwell Museum of Vermont
www.normanrockwellvt.com
Learn about another terrific Rockwell museum. View lots of examples of his artwork.

The Saturday Evening Post: Norman Rockwell Archives
www.saturdayeveningpost.com/sections/art-entertainment/norman-rockwell-art-entertainment
Browse through a large selection of Rockwell's *Post* covers and read interesting facts about each one.

Index

A
aristocracy, 31

B
Boston Public Library, 37

C
Carolus-Duran, 10–12, 15
childhood, 5–9

D
death, 38

E
Edward VII, 34

F
Florence, 5
France, 5, 38

G
Gautreau, Virginie, 20–24
Germany, 5

J
James, Henry, 31

L
London, 24

M
Madame X controversy, 23
Monet, Claude, 31
Morocco, 18
Museum of Fine Arts, Boston, 38

N
nationality, 5, 34, 40

O
Olmstead, Frederick Law, 31

P
Paris, 10, 15, 20, 23–24
poison gas, 38
portraits, 12, 17, 23–24, 26–28, 31–32, 34

R
Rockefeller, John D., 37
Roosevelt, Theodore, 35, 37

S
Salon, the (in Paris), 15, 23
Sargent, Emily (sister), 5, 6
Sargent, FitzWilliam (father), 5
Sargent, Mary (mother), 5, 6
Sargent, Violet (sister), 5
school, 10–12
Spain, 18, 20
Stevenson, Robert Louis, 31

T
technique, 28
travels for inspiration, 18–20
Triumph of Religion, The, 37
Tunisia, 18

U
United States, 12, 14, 34, 37, 40

W
watercolors, 18
Wertheimer family, 31–32
Wilson, Woodrow, 37
World War I, 38

RECEIVED JUN 3 2016